A WOMAN'S GUIDE TO SPIRITUAL WARFARE

Tools for Victorious Living

Volume 1

Sandrarae V. Hyatt

ACKNOWLEDGEMENTS

I render all praise and thanksgiving to my Lord and Savior, Jesus Christ. I give special thanks to my beloved father, the late Pastor Raymond E. Curtis. I also honor my dear, sweet mother, Clydia Mae Curtis; without their foundational teachings of Jesus Christ, spiritual covering, and continued nurturing, I would not be who I am today. Thank you, mom, for all that you have instilled in me. I also give thanks to First Lady Jeanette and Pastor David Curtis for their demonstration of unwavering love and support. To my wonderful husband, John, who supports my spirit of entrepreneurship. Special thanks to our precious gifts from God, our daughters, Jennifer, Teresa, Tiffini, and Jasmine. Your love and laughter makes our hearts smile. I am especially grateful for the love, prayers, encouragement, insight, and friendship of my "sistas," Bridgette, Melissa, Dee, and Mary, I don't know what I would do without them! I thank my brothers, Anthony, June, David, and Danny for their many kindnesses and love. In memory of my deceased brother, Nathaniel, I thank his daughter, Sherita for supporting me in every endeavor! Thank you, baby girl! Thank you to my church family for all the encouraging words spoken in the right season. Thanks to my dear friend, Evangelist Mary Rich. You were a light for me in the darkest years of my life. To my friends, Darlene, Lisa, and Liz, thank you for being listening ears and consistent prayer warriors.

FOREWORD

Asst. Pastor Sandrarae V. Hyatt's *A Woman's Guide to Spiritual Warfare* is a timely, profound message for the body of Christ. It is rare that you find in one person the gift of understanding, wisdom, and knowledge in the Word of God. Sandrarae is such a person. She is a lover of Jesus Christ, and a phenomenal song writer who has the God-given ability to capture innermost secrets of the soul, and give voice to the thoughts of the heart. This book is yet another heavenly work committed to revealing the art of spiritual warfare. I highly recommend and endorse this book as a must-read to all of God's soldiers!

Evangelist Mary Rich
Miracle Revival Tabernacle, East St. Louis, IL

Ephesians 6:11-13

TABLE OF CONTENTS

INTRODUCTION

Why write a book about a woman's guide to spiritual warfare? Historically, a large majority of households had both parents in the home, and men predominantly ruled the households. They were traditionally responsible for providing for their families' well-being, instilling within them a moral compass, and an unshakeable faith in God. After World War I and World War II, more women became heads of households due to men lost in war, social unrest, and social change regarding the roles women began to play in leading their homes. Today, for one reason or another, more and more households are being led by single mothers. They are often required to walk in the shoes of not only mother, but as father, friend, provider, protector, and whatever the circumstances may demand.

As more men began to take a backseat to being spiritual leaders of their homes, women stood in the gap, taking on the roles of priest and prayer warrior. Today, we need more women who will lead and guide their families in the ways of God. In essence, we must learn the art of spiritual warfare to effectively cover ourselves and our families in prayer.

This book in no way denigrates the important roles that men play in carrying out the will of God for their families, churches, or communities. However, it does emphasize that Jesus has issued a clarion call to battle for holy women to stand in the trenches and intercede for the lost souls of men, women, children, families, neighborhoods, communities, churches, leaders, and nations.

God has equipped consecrated women to effectively petition heaven with bull's-eye prayers that overthrow the plans of Satan. If you are bound, oppressed, or defeated, learn how to overcome the enemy by putting on the whole armor of God, believing the word, and speaking what God says about you and your circumstances.

CHAPTER 1

SATAN'S ASSIGNMENT AGAINST WOMEN, WHY ME?

When reading about the fall of man, notice that the first thing Satan did was undermine Eve's faith in God by questioning what God had already commanded. He subtly suggested to Eve that God lied to her about the consequences of disobedience. Satan is using the same tactic today. He wants believers to doubt what God has spoken to them. He wants to convince believers that God is a liar, and cannot be trusted.

When God questioned Eve about her disobedience in eating from the tree of knowledge of good and evil, she exposed the enemy and said, "The serpent beguiled me, and I did eat" (Genesis 3:13). She did not blame God or her husband, but simply confessed the truth and exposed the serpent. The Bible says, "He that covereth his sins shall not prosper: but whoso confesseth and forsaketh *them* shall have mercy" (Proverbs 28:13). God told Satan that he would, put enmity between him and the woman, and between his seed and her seed (Genesis 3:15). All of mankind's redemption rested within Eve's womb. Even though she and Adam were punished for their disobedience, in judgement, God had mercy and blessed them to have a son named Seth. Through his lineage, came the Messiah, Jesus Christ. Since that time, Satan has relentlessly targeted women to abort the call of God upon their lives.

Throughout history, the destiny of world leaders, generation changers, and kingdom champions have been secretly hidden within the wombs of God's daughters, divinely orchestrated to be birthed in their appointed season according to the plans and purposes of the Almighty.

Please understand, Satan hates all of mankind, but has a particular hatred toward women. Why? I can think of a few more reasons. God specially created women to have the capability of carrying and birthing the precious souls of children into the world. Every child has the propensity to have authority over Satan and bruise his head. Jesus said, "I give unto you power to tread on serpents and scorpions, and over all the power of the enemy" (Luke 10:19). The seed of mankind are deadly threats to the kingdom of darkness. King Herod did everything in his power to abort the destiny of Jesus by killing all male children two years old and under. But Jesus was safely hidden within Mary's womb, wrapped in human flesh to carry out the incredible assignment of man's redemption.

CHAPTER 2

YOU ARE IN THE NINTH MONTH!

Make up your mind today that you will not forfeit nor abort your destiny. Within your womb, you carry the precious cargo of souls, resources, dreams, and gifts ready to be birthed at such a time as this. The reason you are going through such intense adversity is because you are in the ninth month. This is why the enemy has been throwing so many things at you. You are about to give birth. Get positioned to bring forth. *Hold on. Bear down. Focus,* now *breathe.* The Lord is walking you through it. Yes, it is difficult. Yes, there is pain. Yes, you are tired, but deliverance is nigh. *Push.* You are about to hear the wonderful sound of realized dreams, and embrace the unfolding reality of God's promises!

Just as a physician gives specific instructions to ensure a safe, healthy pregnancy and delivery, so does our heavenly Father. God gives his people specific instructions for every trial we face. The battle that you are facing right now is already won. Listen for the voice of God to provide and equip you with divine, strategic impartation and revelation to obtain victory over your enemy. The battle that you are in will not be won by fighting in your flesh. Your battle will not be won by mere human efforts. The Bible says, "Do not fear or be dismayed because of this great multitude, for the battle is not yours but God's" (2 Chronicles 20:15). Praise God! This is a rhema word for somebody today.

When David faced Goliath, he prophesied the giant's defeat. David told Goliath, "This day will the Lord deliver thee into mine hand; and I will smite thee, and take thine head from thee; and I will give the carcasses of the host of the Philistines this day unto the fowls of the air, and to the wild beasts of the earth; that all the earth may know that there is a God in Israel" (1 Samuel 17:46). Prophesy to the enemy, declare that he is a defeated foe, and that God is with you. Let him know that no weapon formed will prosper against you!

I remember a time in my life when I was ready to abort the destiny Jesus planned for me. For more nights than I care to remember, torment sat at the table of my soul. I was afraid to face the morning, and dreaded the approaching evening. Fear greeted me when I woke up, and taunted me when it was time to sleep. I was a mere shell of the vibrant, confident young lady that I once knew. What happened to me? How did I arrive at this place? I listened to the lies of the enemy, and deliberately chose to turn my back on God to see what the world had to offer. I found myself alone, very much alone. Emptiness, fear, abandonment, and rejection filled every room of my heart. I began to cry out to the Lord to save me, and I am so glad He did. He received my backslidden soul with warm, open arms. I am so grateful that Jesus extended his mercy, forgave me, and loved me. He will do the same for you!

Though I was born again, I still needed complete wholeness for the hidden, emotional wounds of my past. There were some things in my past that I really regretted doing. It opened up a door of fear in my life. There were times when I wondered if I would ever be free. I viewed myself as a vulnerable, weak, victim. I envisioned myself as unprotected prey for the enemy to attack at will.

This is the image the devil wanted me to see and believe. He wanted me to think that God did not hear my prayers, and that He would not save me from the enemy. Whenever the enemy would attack me, I would begin to desperately call more "seasoned" saints who I thought could get a prayer through. I had very little faith that my prayers would be answered or heard. For a long time, I lived in fear that I would never be good enough or "saved" enough for the Lord. I carried so much guilt from day to day. I felt guilty about not trusting the Lord enough. I felt guilty because my faith was not strong enough. I felt guilty because I entertained bad thoughts. Get the picture?

I felt like I just could not live up to God's word. Therefore, I was constantly questioning my standing with God. I frequently wondered if I was being punished for past sins. These were all lies from the devil. Do you hear what I am saying? I know the devil is telling you the same lies. We cannot earn our way into salvation. Salvation is a gift from God that we receive by faith and grace, not good works.

The word says, "For it is God which worketh in you both to will and to do of *his* good pleasure" (Philippians 2:13). Through the power and guidance of the Holy Spirit, He teaches us how to live in the Spirit. "For in him we live, and move, and have our being" (Acts 17:28). Let go, and let God have His way. Yield yourself to Him in childlike faith, and trust that He will mold and make you into His image.

The Bible says, "There is therefore now no condemnation to those who are in Christ Jesus." His grace does not give us the license to sin, but the comfort in knowing if we do sin, we have an advocate, Jesus Christ, who makes intercession for us. He knows our frailties. If we sin, saints, let us go boldly before the throne of grace to obtain mercy and grace to help in time of need. Repent, and ask the Lord to help you in areas of weakness. He is longsuffering, and His mercies are new every morning.

The more Satan afflicted and attacked me, the more I grew. The more I got in the word, the more the word got in me. Jesus did not want me to live in fear, so He began to train me in the art of spiritual warfare. The first thing I learned is to believe God's word, and reject every lie.

CHAPTER 3

THE ABC'S OF FAITH

Now faith is the substance of things hoped for, the evidence of things not seen (Hebrews 11:1). Faith is unwavering belief in the reality of something and/or someone. The reason I did not think God heard my prayers was because I did not really believe God's word. Oh, it is easy to quote scriptures, but it is quite another thing to actually believe when it feels like your world is reeling out of control. Our faith cannot be based on our emotions or what we see. Faith is not a feeling, but a choice to believe. Just simply choose to believe. Whose report will you believe?

Where Does Faith Come From?
Where does faith come from? Our faith comes from God. The word of God teaches that He has given "everyman a measure of faith (Romans 12:3). You may be under the assumption that you have no faith, but this scripture clearly states that we have been given a measure of faith. Don't allow the enemy to torment your mind about not having enough faith. Jesus is the "author and finisher of our faith." "He that has begun a good work in us shall perform it until the day of Christ" (Philippians 1:6). Jesus knows all about our faith, and what He plans to do to increase it.

Stretching the Muscles of Faith

As I stated earlier, fear began affecting me in different areas of my life. If my sinuses were making me feel bad, I would stay at home. If I chose to go somewhere, the sinus problems would quickly and significantly intensify. Whenever I would go to the store, fear would assault me. I would quickly leave the store, and go sit in the car to regain my composure. I would feel so defeated. I had to make up my mind that either I was going to believe God and His word, or not. I began to try God at His word.

At first, it seemed like things were not changing, but oh behind the scenes, our great, big God was working it out for me. When the devil would taunt me, and say that things would never change, the Holy Ghost would encourage me to press forward. I intentionally believed and purposed in my heart that, "I can do all things through Christ who strengthens me." After a while, the Lord blessed me to go into the store without being accosted by the spirit of fear. As I began to believe and rely upon God's word, the chains that once held me captive began to fall off. Praise God!

I had to fight against giving in to the temptation of allowing emotions of fear, worry, anxiety, and dread rule my day-to-day existence. I had to fight against the barrage of lies that Satan would use to assault my mind. I could not afford to consider how I felt in my body. I daily asked the Lord to give me strength and peace in my body, soul, and spirit to keep moving forward. And He did just that.

One of the benefits of stretching our natural muscles is that it helps increase flexibility and range. The Lord stretches our spiritual muscles to help increase our flexibility and range of trusting Him. The thought and dread of fear is no longer a part of my shopping experience. I am made free by the precious blood of Christ. Praise God! Hallelujah! God is a deliverer! God is faithful. You, too, can depend on God and His word.

The enemy would have you believe that you will never be free from fear, depression, anxiety, brokenness, low self-esteem, or whatever issue you may be facing. Nothing could be further from the truth. Don't you dare believe that lie. Jesus said that He came to set the captives free. It is not a mere coincidence that you are reading this book at this particular season in your life. This is your season to break free from every shackle and bondage that has ever enslaved you. Choose to believe God's word over the lies of the enemy, and watch your life transform before your very eyes.

The Recipe of Faith and Works

The Lord taught me that believing the word is not enough. What? Faith alone is not enough. James 2:14-17 says, "What doth it profit, my brethren, though a man say he hath faith, and have not works? Can faith save him? If a brother or sister be naked, and destitute of daily food, And one of you say unto them, Depart in peace, be ye warmed and filled; notwithstanding ye give them not those things which are needful to the body; what doth it profit? Even so faith, if it hath not works, is dead, being alone." Knowing that a person needs something to eat, but not taking action to provide what they need is useless. Therefore, knowing and believing God's word is futile, if we do not take action to do what the word says. Believe what Jesus says about you, and take a leap of faith by standing on His word.

Jesus told Peter, "Launch out into the deep, and let down your nets for a draught. And Simon answering said unto him, Master, we have toiled all the night, and have taken nothing: nevertheless at thy word I will let down the net. And when they had this done, they enclosed a great multitude of fishes: and their net brake." Simon Peter told Jesus, "Lord, we worked all night trying to catch fish, but haven't caught a thing. Nevertheless, I will do it at your word." Peter was willing to take a leap of faith at Jesus' word and launch out into the deep.

When the enemy says, you can't live a life without worry or fear, take a leap of faith and launch out into the deep. Tell the devil that God has not given you the spirit of fear, but of power, love, and a sound mind. When thoughts of fear and worry attack your mind, take action and resist the devil. This is faith with works. Along with our faith, we need to speak to our circumstances. Jesus illustrated the perfect example of speaking to circumstances when he cursed a fig tree.

"Now in the morning as he returned into the city, he hungered. And when he saw a fig tree in the way, he came to it, and found nothing thereon, but leaves only, and said unto it, let no fruit grow on thee henceforward forever. And presently the fig tree withered away. And when the disciples saw it, they marveled, saying, how soon is the fig tree withered away! Jesus answered and said unto them, Verily I say unto you, If ye have faith, and doubt not, ye shall not only do this which is done to the fig tree, but also if ye shall say unto this mountain, Be thou removed, and be thou cast into the sea; it shall be done. And all things, whatsoever ye shall ask in prayer, believing, ye shall receive" (Matthew 21:18-22).

Jesus cursed the fig tree, and immediately, it was dried from the root at the word of Jesus. Jesus said, "Whosoever shall say unto this mountain." Take notice that Jesus did not complain about the tree not having fruit, but spoke directly to the tree and decreed that it would not ever bring forth fruit. With faith in God, speak to the mountains of your life. Without doubting, tell the mountain to be removed and cast into the sea. Saints, we need to believe God and speak the word of Christ to every mountain in our life. "Death and life is in the power of the tongue, and they that love it shall eat the fruit thereof" (Proverbs 18:21). Isaiah 55:11 says, "So shall my word be that goeth forth out of my mouth: it shall not return unto me void, but it shall accomplish that which I please, and it shall prosper *in the thing* whereto I sent it." God cannot lie, and His word is true. Let us endeavor to frame our worlds with the unfailing word of God.

Testify, Testify, Testify!

There are things in our lives that need to be cursed from the root. When we speak words into the atmosphere, it has the capability of either bringing forth death or life. To any person reading this book, in the name of Jesus, I bind and speak death to every spirit of fear, anxiety, dread, anger, all generational curses, or low self-esteem from the root right now. In the name of Jesus, I curse the manifestations of these spirits and all their roots, fruits, tentacles, seeds, and command them to die now!

In the name of Jesus, you are loosed from every evil spirit, and all their roots, fruits, tentacles, and seeds; for Jesus Christ makes you free! He whom the Son has made free is free indeed. Tell the devil he has no place in your life; your body is the temple of the Holy Ghost and no unclean thing shall dwell therein. Revelation 12:11 says, "And they overcame him by the blood of the Lamb, and by the word of their testimony; and they loved not their lives unto the death." We overcome Satan by the blood of the Lamb, and the word of our testimony. Testify of what God's word says about your situation. Speak God's word into the atmosphere!

CHAPTER 4

SHUT THE DOOR

For me, sinus problems were an open door that Satan used to bring in fear and anxiety. The sinus symptoms would make me feel so drained in my body, until I became very fearful. Of course, the enemy would magnify the symptoms by presenting fearful thoughts and images. It seemed I had no control over the sinus issues or the enemy. Things got so bad until I did not want to attend social functions. As soon as I would awake, Satan would bring thoughts and images of me being weak, defeated, and sick. For a while, I accepted those ideas, and that is how my day would go. I would speak those ideas into the atmosphere and feel weak, defeated, and sick.

One day, the Lord revealed to me that when those negatives thoughts come to mind, I must cast those thoughts down and replace them with what His word says about me. I began to say, "In the name of Jesus, I bind every evil spirit that comes against me." "In the name of Jesus, I pull down strongholds, cast down imaginations, and every high thing that exalts itself against the knowledge of God; bringing into captivity every thought to the obedience of Christ." "In the name of Jesus, I shut every satanic door in my life, and seal it shut with the blood of Christ." "In the name of Jesus,

I decree, declare, and testify by the blood of the Lamb that I am loosed from every evil spirit, and wrong thinking." "He whom the Son has made free, is free indeed." "With the stripes of Jesus I am healed." It is important to exercise caution about what we allow or entertain in our minds. Sometimes, we unknowingly open demonic doors into our lives. It can be things we read, or watch on television. It can even be the company we keep. Shut the door, and keep the enemy out!

Praying God's Will
John 5:14-15 says, "And this is the confidence that we have in him, that, if we ask any thing according to his will, he heareth us: And if we know that he hear us, whatsoever we ask, we know that we have the petitions that we desired of him." Our confidence should not be placed in our circumstances or in the lies of the enemy. Our confidence should be placed in Jesus and His word. Freedom from fear is God's will for our lives. Therefore, when we ask to be made free from fear, (or other negative behaviors) we are praying the will of God. Because we know that it is His will, we know that He hears, and has granted our petition. We already have the victory!

The Waiting Room
The next principal was learning how to wait patiently for the manifestation of the answer of petitioned prayers in the physical realm. The Bible gives us clear instructions on how to wait upon the Lord. One passage says, "Rest in the Lord and wait patiently for him" (Psalm 37:7). Resting in the Lord means that we are peacefully trusting Jesus. We are not moved by what we see or hear, because we have absolute trust that Jesus will bring us out. Be still, and know that I am God. Still your mind. Cease from all frantic activity, and wait on the Lord. We so often try to take matters into or own hands because, in essence, we are saying that we don't trust God to do it. We are really saying that we know what is best for us.

Isaiah 40:31 says, "They that wait upon the Lord shall renew their strength; they shall mount up with wings as eagles; they shall run, and not be weary; and they shall walk, and not faint." In this life, we encounter heartache, pain, and affliction. Sometimes the burden is so great we become weary in our minds and bodies. You see, we cannot successfully go through this life without the strength and peace of Christ. Jesus said, "My peace give I unto thee."

Another passage says, "He gives us strength and peace." "Many are the afflictions of the righteous, but the Lord delivers him out of them all." "Come unto me, all *ye* that labour and are heavy laden, and I will give you rest" (Matthew 11:28). See, I had an idea of how I wanted the Lord to deliver me. I envisioned a mighty, anointed man or woman of God laying hands on me in the height of the service, and being instantly transformed from all that oppressed me. Now that could happen, and sometimes it does happen that way. However, Jesus wanted me to come to Him for deliverance. He desired that my trust be in Him and not in man. There is nothing wrong with asking saints for prayers, but rely solely upon Jesus to do the work in His time and in His way. "We are his workmanship created in Christ Jesus unto good works," (Ephesians 2:10). It is His responsibility to provide everything we need as His sheep, and He is willing and able to deliver us from all evil. Jesus delivered me in His time and His way.

Praise and Worship Shift the Atmosphere
While waiting on the Lord, He taught me how to rejoice in Him. I began thanking God for the things He already did for me. I began thanking Him for the ways He's already made. I began praising Him for the times He delivered me from harm's way. As I began to worship and praise, the Lord would lift my spirit and outlook on life. When we begin to praise and worship our Lord, we invite His sweet presence into our atmosphere. "Where the Spirit of the Lord is, there is liberty" (2 Corinthians 3:16). We are literally inviting

God's kingdom to come and His will to be done on earth as it is in heaven. Soon my problems were no longer the focus of my mind. Day by day, I became stronger and stronger through the power of the Holy Spirit. God is no respecter of persons. He did it for me; he will do it for you too. The Old Testament provides a beautiful story of how God honored the worship and prayer of a heartbroken woman named Hannah.

CHAPTER 5

HANNAH, PRAYER WARRIOR

There are several examples of women petitioning heaven for themselves, their families and even nations. Hannah is a prime example of how to engage in spiritual warfare to obtain deliverances in difficult situations. Hannah was one of two wives married to Elkanah, a Levite. It is believed that Hannah was the primary wife, but could not bear children. The Bible says, "God had shut her womb" (1 Samuel 1:6). Penninah was the name of the other wife. Penninah was very fruitful, and was blessed to have children. Each year they would travel from the hill country of Ephraim to the temple in Shiloh to worship and give a sacrifice unto the Lord. Year after year, when going to the tabernacle, Penninah would cruelly taunt Hannah regarding her infertility until she was reduced to tears. Along with the despair of being childless, and Penninah's relentless harassment, Hannah's heart would break over and over again. Although her husband loved her dearly, he could not understand the unbearable grief she experienced because of not being able to conceive her very own child. Hannah knew that only God could satisfy the insatiable yearning within to have a child.

Delay Does Not Mean Denial

The story goes on to say that "her adversary also provoked her sore, for to make her fret, because the LORD had shut up her womb. And as he did so year by year, when she went up to the house of the LORD, so she provoked her; therefore she wept, and did not eat" (1 Samuel 1:6-7). No doubt, the adversary knew that God was the one who shut her womb. Penninah used this information as a weapon to wound and torment Hannah. Penninah may have taunted her by saying, "This God you worship and sacrifice to is the one responsible for your womb being closed." She may have told Hannah that she was not a "real" woman since she could not have children. Penninah may have gone so far as to say that Elkanah married her because Hannah could not give him children.

Our enemy does not play fair! What womb or door has Christ closed in your life that the enemy taunts you about? Have opportunities of obtaining a promotion, relationship, home, or car been closed to you at this season of your life? What lies is the enemy whispering in your ear to persuade you to stop trusting God? Though the Lord was well able to open Hannah's womb, it was not the season. Ecclesiastes tells us that there is a time and a season for everything under the sun. Her enemy knew that this was an agonizing cross for Hannah to bear. Little did Hannah know that not only was God going to bless her to have children, but she was about to birth one of the greatest prophets into the kingdom of God! Learning to wait patiently for the Lord, and not fretting about anything is key. Remember, delay is not denial. God did not say that her situation was a permanent fixture in her life. There was a time and a season for Hannah's situation to shift. There is a time and a season for our situations to shift as well!

Breakthrough

Notice that the scripture enlightens us about the strategic timing of the enemy's attack. Take notice that each year while on their way to worship God, Hannah's enemy would provoke and torment her, and every year Hannah would become depressed and distraught. The enemy will try to hinder you from worshiping because in your worship is your breakthrough! What situation in your life is the enemy taunting you with year after year because God has closed a door that you want open? There was a time and a season for Hannah's prayer to be answered. The same is true for you and me!

Is the enemy tormenting your mind with thoughts of God failing you? In what areas of your life are you stuck? The enemy has not changed this tactic. No doubt, Hannah was oppressed by a spirit of anxiety, evil foreboding, despair, and depression each time they journeyed to worship and sacrifice.

However, one particular year, the Bible says that Hannah got up after eating and drinking in Shiloh. One day she got up from her place of pain, went into the temple of the Lord, and prayed and wept before the Lord of hosts. She got up from her place of self-pity; she got up from being a victim; she got up from her past; she got up from her fears; she got up from her tears; she got up from her frustrations. Hannah poured her heart out to the Lord about all of her troubles.

The word of God teaches us to cast all our cares upon Him because He cares for us. Instead of allowing depression to sit at the table of her mind, Hannah made a decision to call upon the name of the Lord. Nowhere else in the story is it previously mentioned that she called upon the Lord. Men should always pray, and not to faint. Pray without ceasing. As Hannah spoke to the Lord in her heart, the priest, Eli, assumed she was drunk. She shared with Eli that she was not drunk, but was pouring out her soul unto the Lord.

Hannah did not get angry nor insulted by the priest's assumption. She did not give up hope and leave the temple because the man of God thought she was drunk. She continued in prayer. How often do we miss out on our blessings and breakthroughs because someone at church offends us? The priest didn't know the pain of her past. In spite of what people think about us, we have to press forward and in utter abandonment call upon the name of the Lord. When she informed Eli that she was crying out to the Lord, He spoke to her and said, "Go in peace; and may the God of Israel grant your petition that you have asked of Him" (1 Samuel 1:17).

Hannah prayed until she received a rhema word from the Lord. She prayed until she was no longer sad. She prayed until she got a breakthrough. She laid aside the garments of heaviness and put on the garments of praise. Hannah was assured in her spirit that God would give her the desires of her heart. After she prayed, they all got up early the next morning and worshipped before departing for home. In other words, after she prayed and made supplication unto the Lord, she worshipped. After we have emptied the cares of our heart unto the Lord, we need to worship. Honor God, reverence Him, give thanks unto His holy name.

One Word from the Lord Changes Everything
That morning Hannah had a new spring in her step. She had a new attitude. One word from the Lord changed her entire mindset. One word from the Lord changed her entire atmosphere. One word from the Lord changed her entire life. She believed the word of the Lord. The word says, "Believe ye the Lord so shall you be established. Believe ye also the prophet, so shall you prosper" (2 Chronicles 20:20). She believed the Lord, and she believed the prophet.

When they got home, Elkanah and Hannah came together as husband and wife, and the Lord remembered Hannah. The Lord opened Hannah's womb in His time and season, and she conceived a son named Samuel. Jesus remembered Hannah's prayer, and honored her request. Not only did the Lord bless her to give birth to Samuel, but she gave birth to three sons and two daughters. God will do exceeding abundantly above all that we ask or think. Hannah's effectual fervent prayers availed much and gave her the desires of her heart.

Wake Up and Shake Yourself Loose!

Just as Hannah took off her garments of heaviness and put on garments of praise, so must we. "Awake, awake; put on your strength, O Zion; put on your beautiful garments, O Jerusalem, the holy city: for from now on there shall no more come into you the uncircumcised and the unclean. Shake yourself from the dust; arise, and sit down, O Jerusalem: loose yourself from the bands of your neck, O captive daughter of Zion" (Isaiah 52:1-2). Are you ready?

Let us awake out of the stupor of complacency, and put on the garments of praise. Let us shake ourselves loose from the dust of regret, fear, disappointment, failure, mistakes, and sin. Arise, get up, from all that has hurt or wounded us. Take your rightful place. For the word teaches that we are seated in heavenly places. Let us lay aside every weight and the sin that does so easily beset us. Let us look unto Jesus, the Author and Finisher of our faith. If we plan to live in peace, we must be dressed for war.

CHAPTER 6
WEAPONS OF MASS DESTRUCTION

Our daily battle is against an unseen enemy who relentlessly seeks to kill, steal, and destroy in every area of our lives. Though it seems that flesh and blood is warring against us, the reality is that we are wrestling "against principalities, against powers, against the rulers of the darkness of this world, against spiritual wickedness in high places" (Ephesians 6:12). Our enemy cannot be fought with guns and knives, but we can successfully overcome the enemy by our faith and the proper spiritual attire. In order to destroy the works of the enemy, we must put on the whole armor of God. Prior to engaging the enemy in battle, soldiers are required to suit up with special attire. The same concept applies to believers.

The suit of armor we wear is an impenetrable, specially designed, protective covering that shields us from the attacks of our enemy, and ensures victory! Romans 13:14 instructs us to "Put on the Lord Jesus Christ, and make no provision for the flesh in regard to its lusts." Ephesian 6:10-18 equips the soldier of God so that we might stand firm when the enemy comes against us. Ephesians 6:11 says, "Put on the whole armor of God, that ye may be able to stand against the wiles of the devil." The Lord Jesus requires that we put on the whole armor of God, not part of it. How can we expect victory if we are half-dressed? If we go into battle with our shoes on but no helmet, we afford the enemy an opportunity to land a deadly blow. Let's examine each piece of armor and its purpose.

Our spiritual armor consists of seven vital weapons that are imperative for victory. These weapons complement one another. Our loins are girded with truth, we have on the breastplate of righteousness, our feet are shod with the preparation of the gospel of peace, we take the shield of faith, the helmet of salvation, the sword of the Spirit, and fervent prayer (Ephesian 6:14-18).

Loins

A man's loins were considered the seat of his strength and stamina. The loins may refer to the genital area, groin, hips, or lower abdomen. In ancient times, men and women both wore long tunics. The difference was that men's tunics stopped at about the knee, and women's tunics were longer. If men were required to perform a task, they had to gather the tunic to keep it from getting in the way. This was their way of gathering their garments around their loins. We, too, must gather the truth of God's word around the loins of our heart. What is truth?

- Let us take a look at the scriptures below:
- I am the Way, the Truth, and the Light (John 14:6).
- Sanctify them through thy truth; your word is truth (John 17:17).
- Lead me in your truth and teach me, for you are the God of my salvation; for you I wait all the day long (Psalm 25:5).
- Send out your light and your truth; let them lead me; let them bring me to your holy hill and to your dwelling (Psalm 43:3).

- Teach me your way, O LORD, that I may walk in your truth; unite my heart to fear your name (Psalm 86:11).

So, Jesus said to the Jews who had believed in Him, "If you abide in my word, you are truly my disciples, and you will know the allowed to grow in our hearts, they insidiously invade every aspect of our lives and hinder spiritual development. We become weighed down with the cares of this world. Jesus instructed his disciples to guard their hearts, because out of the heart proceeds evil thoughts, murder, adultery, all sexual immorality, theft, lying, and slander (Matthew 15:19).

We are the righteousness of God and are expected to let the word of God cleanse our hearts and minds from all filthiness of the flesh and of the spirit. We should cry out to God, "Create in us a clean heart and renew a right spirit within us" (Psalm 51:10). We are commanded to put on the breastplate of faith and love. Faith is the shield that protects us from the darts of the enemy, and love covers a multitude of sins. Colossians 3:14 says, "... And above all these things put on charity (love), which is the bond of perfectness."

Feet Shod with the Preparation of the Gospel of Peace

What does it mean to have our feet shod with the preparation of the gospel of peace? The word, "shod" means to wear footgear or a covering for the feet. The gospel of peace is the good news that Jesus died on the cross to save a dying world from their sins, and has granted every person an opportunity to have eternal life. A soldier need shoes on to protect his feet from stones, glass, or debris. When the feet are not covered, they are exposed to the elements that may allow opportunity for injury to the feet. Just as natural shoes allow us to walk on the ground without fear of injury, so also, our spiritual shoes shod with the word of God help us to walk upon the difficult places of life, and face the enemy with sure-footed stability. The Lord makes our feet like hinds' feet so we can effectively walk upon our high places (Psalm 18:33).

Luke 10:19-20 says, "Behold, I give you the authority to trample on serpents and scorpions, and over all the power of the enemy, and nothing shall by any means hurt you" (Luke 10:19). Jesus Christ has equipped us with power to walk over Satan and all His principalities and power. Isaiah 54:17 says, "No weapon that is formed against you shall prosper; and every tongue that shall rise against you in judgment you shall condemn. This is the heritage of the servants of the LORD, and their righteousness is of me, said the LORD." This clearly informs us that weapons will be formed, but they shall not prosper against the people of God.

The Shield of Faith
None of the other weapons are more highly exalted than the shield of faith because faith is the foundation upon which our entire salvation rests. The word of God teaches that without faith it is impossible to please God. 1 John 5:4 says, "For whatsoever is born of God overcomes the world: and this is the victory that overcomes the world, even our Faith." Faith is having complete confidence in someone or something. Faith is believing and trusting God; it is trust at rest. "Faith is the substance of things hoped for, the evidence of things not seen" (Hebrews 11:1). When the enemy sends his fiery darts of lies and temptation, the shield of faith extinguishes every dart. The shield of faith is impenetrable to any weapon that Satan attempts to employ. In the famous Star Trek series, Captain Kirk would say, "Shields up" when bracing themselves for an attack from the Klingons. Shields up, saints!

The Helmet of Salvation
Helmets are designed to protect the body's most valuable asset, the brain. This is a parallel truth in regards to the believer's helmet of salvation. It is important that we wear the helmet of salvation

to guard our minds from the lies, deceptions, and temptations of the enemy. The word teaches that we have the mind of Christ. The word, "salvation," means to salvage or deliver. The word tells us we have been delivered from the kingdom of darkness, and translated into the kingdom of God's dear Son (Colossians 1:13).

Simply put, we have been saved from eternal damnation. We have been accepted into the beloved. We can receive tremendous hope and comfort by focusing on the incredible sacrifice Christ made to save us. This hope works like a helmet to protect our minds from the discouragement and despair in this world. Though we are in the world, we are not of the world. We have the mind of Christ, and our ways of living and thinking should be different than the world (Philippians 2:5). God's laws should be written on our hearts and minds so that we do not sin against Him. The scripture teaches, "I do not pray that You should take them out of the world, but that You should keep them from the evil one. They are not of the world, just as I am not of the world" (John 17:15-16). No matter what the enemy is telling you, know that you have on the helmet of salvation; you are a new creature in Christ. Your mind is new, and the old way of thinking is passed away. You now have a new way of thinking.

Sword of the Spirit
History tells us that soldiers used swords to engage their enemies in close combat. It is said that the swords of Roman soldiers were so powerful, that they were able to pierce through metal. We are soldiers for the Captain of the Host, and wield the word of God as an effective, lethal weapon against our enemies. Hebrews 4:12 says, "For the word of God is quick, and powerful, and sharper than two-edged sword, piercing even to the dividing asunder of soul and spirit, and of the joints and marrow, and is a discerner of the thoughts and intents of the heart." Jesus is the Word! Speak the word to decree and declare victory! Don't rely upon your emotions, but believe God. John 1:1 says, "In the beginning was the Word,

and the Word was with God, and the Word was God." Romans 10:8 says, "The word is nigh thee, even in thy mouth, and in thy heart: that is, the word of faith, which we preach." Speaking the word of God brings about change in our atmosphere or situation.

Praying and Watching

Jesus taught His disciples to watch and pray to avoid entering into temptation. This does not mean for us to be anxious, but vigilant upon our watch, and always, always pray without ceasing. Let us be mindful of what we look at on television, watch the things that we think about, watch what we say, watch who we keep company with, etc. Watching is only part of the command. We are also required to pray along with our watching that we do not fall prey to sin.

A good soldier understands the importance of being vigilant and prayerful. We are soldiers for Christ, and our goal should be to keep His commandments.

Committed to Christ

Soldiers must be committed to following orders from their captain even when they don't fully understand the orders. This means that their minds must be free from the clutter of fear, doubt, and unbelief. We are soldiers and must trust Jesus, the Captain of our salvation, enough to know that He will not send us into a battle that we cannot win. The scripture says, "But thanks be to God, which giveth us the victory through our Lord Jesus" (1 Corinthians 15:57). Christ has equipped us with everything we need to consistently experience victory.

As previously stated, our minds need to be cleansed of all fear, doubt, and unbelief. How do we accomplish this challenging feat when everything around us seems to be the complete opposite of what God has promised? We accomplish this by saturating our minds with the word of God. We accomplish it by hearing the word of God, speaking the word of God, and believing the word of God.

CHAPTER 7
KNOWING WHO WE ARE IN CHRIST

It is absolutely imperative that we know who we are in Christ Jesus and recognize our authority in Him to pull down strongholds in our minds, cast down imaginations and every high thing that exalts itself against the knowledge of God, and bring every thought into captivity unto the obedience of Christ. "For though we walk in the flesh, we do not war after the flesh: (For the weapons of our warfare are not carnal, but mighty through God to the pulling down of strong holds;) Casting down imaginations, and every high thing that exalteth itself against the knowledge of God, and bringing into captivity every thought to the obedience of Christ; And having in a readiness to revenge all disobedience, when your obedience is fulfilled" (2 Corinthians 10:3-6).

The amplified version says, "Our weapons are divinely powerful for the destruction of fortresses. We are destroying sophisticated arguments and every exalted and proud thing that sets itself up against the [true] knowledge of God, and we are taking every thought and purpose captive to the obedience of Christ, being ready to punish every act of disobedience, when your own obedience [as a church] is complete" (2 Corinthians 10:3-6). We simply must believe God, and the word that He has given us.

When we don't know who we are in Christ, we are prone to become enslaved again with the yoke of bondage. Some of us have been through horrendous trials and pain. Some of us have been beaten, abused, betrayed, molested, rejected, abandoned, and mistreated by the very people that were supposed to love, nurture, and protect us. When we fall prey to these kinds of circumstances, the enemy uses the occasion as an inroad to undermine our identity.

Experiences of this kind are capable of eating away at our self-esteem, our self-view, and how we perceive God. It opens demonic doorways to fear, anxiety, dread, and a range of negative strongholds in the mind. The enemy's plan is for us to continue to see ourselves as victims of our circumstances. We have to know that we are not what we have been through.

This is the same tactic that Satan used against the children of Israel centuries ago when God delivered them with a mighty hand of deliverance out of the land of Egypt. God Almighty stripped Egypt of their power and authority over the Israelites. After God led them from Pharaoh and out of the land of Egypt, Pharaoh decided to pursue them. Don't think the enemy is going to let you go without a fight. You've got to know who you are. Although the Lord delivered them out of their circumstances, they still saw themselves as powerless slaves. How many of us have been delivered from various strongholds, impossible situations, but still see ourselves as slaves or victims to these things?

Another example of God's people not realizing who they were, was when the Israelites stood on the threshold of entering into the Promised Land. Spies were sent to scout out the land. The spies scouted the land, and reported that the land was just like the Lord promised, but there were giants in the land. In their sight, they saw themselves as grasshoppers in comparison to the giants in the land. They were looking at the wrong picture. They forgot the miraculous wonders God performed while they were yet in Egypt. They did not trust that God would keep His promises. What about you? Are you struggling to trust God to handle the giants in your life? Do you have a distorted view of your identity in Christ?

Identity Theft

They were experiencing spiritual identity theft. Identity theft occurs when there has been a breach in security. When firewalls are not securely in place, it allows hackers to get into the computer system and steal your identity. By entertaining lies of the enemy, we allow the enemy to steal our spiritual identity or re-program our hard drive. Once security is breached, the enemy attempts to hardwire unforgiveness, fear, and bitterness in our hearts. This is why it is imperative to guard our hearts.

Some of us are like the children of Israel. Though we are born-again believers in Christ Jesus, we have been listening to the lies of the enemy. Maybe your family told you that you would never be anything but a slave to drugs or alcoholism. Maybe they told you that you were better off dead. I am here to remind you of who we are in Christ Jesus. I am here to remind you that we are daughters of the King of Kings and Lord of Lords. With that comes special privileges, power, and authority. The Lord not only requires that we know Him, but that we know who we are in Him.

The word of God teaches that if any man be in Christ, he is a new creature. Old things are passed away, behold all things become new. The person that we used to be no longer exists. We are a completely new creation. When the enemy tries to remind you of what or who you used to be, rebuke him, and declare that you are a new creation in Christ Jesus. "God has delivered us from the kingdom of darkness and translated us into the kingdom of His Dear Son, Jesus" (Colossians 1:13). The moment we accepted Jesus as our Lord and Savior, we became new creatures.

However, Satan wants to convince us that we have not really changed at all. He wants us to believe that we are the same defeated, hopeless people of our past. One of his goals is to convince us that God will fail us. However, the Lord has told us that He would never leave us nor forsake us. Immersing ourselves in the word of God, and letting the power of the word take root in our hearts will effectively combat the lies of the enemy. We must continually believe what the word of God says about our identity. Begin to decree, declare, and testify by the blood of the Lamb that you are who God says you are.

Below is a list of declarations that speak of who we are in Christ Jesus:

- I have put off the old man and have put on the new man, which is renewed in knowledge after the image of Him who created me (Colossians 3:9-10).
- I am no longer fearful, because God has not given me a spirit of fear, but of power, love, and of a sound mind (2 Timothy 1:7).
- We are His workmanship, created in Christ Jesus unto good works (Ephesians 2:10).
- We are redeemed from the curse of the law of sin and death (Galatians 3:13).
- I am saved by grace through faith (Ephesians 2:8).
- My body is the temple of the Holy Spirit (1Corinthians 6:19).
- I am protected because the Angel of the Lord is encamped around about me (Psalm 34:7).
- I am an heir and joint heir through Christ Jesus (Romans 8:17).
- I have the mind of Christ (1 Corinthians 2:16).
- I have received the gift of righteousness and I reign as a king and priest in life by Jesus Christ (Romans 5:17).
- I have received the keys to the kingdom of heaven, and whatsoever I bind on earth shall be bound in heaven,

and whatsoever I loose on earth shall be loosed in heaven (Matthew 16:19).

- I am more than a conqueror through Him who loves me (Romans 8:37).

These declarations are just a small portion of the many truths about who we have become through faith in Christ Jesus. There are many more declarations and promises in the holy scriptures for every adversity you may face. Search the scriptures, and add to this list. Let the word of Christ dwell richly within you. In addition to knowing who we are in Christ, we need to know and understand who Christ is.

Knowing Our Father

Who is your father? What is your last name? The answers to these questions are all identifying factors of who you belong to and who you are. Names speak of your lineage, culture, status, and power. As believers, it is imperative that we recognize who we belong to. A key component in spiritual warfare is really knowing our heavenly Father, His Son, Jesus Christ, and the Holy Spirit.

Below are just a few names of our heavenly Father:

- El Shaddai (Lord God Almighty)
- Adonai (Lord, Master)
- Jehovah-Raah (The Lord my Shepherd)
- Jehovah-Rapha (The Lord that heals)
- Jehovah-Jireh (The Lord will provide)
- Jehovah-Shalom (The Lord is peace)
- Yahweh Sabbaoth (The Lord of Hosts)

As you can see, the God we serve is everything we need. He has given us His Son as the propitiation (provision for forgiveness) for our sins, and has given Him a name above all names. His name is Jesus. The Bible says, "For God so loved the world that He gave his only begotten Son, that whosoever believeth in Him shall not perish, but have everlasting life" (John 3:16). We serve a mighty God who thinks so much of us that He was willing to sacrifice His only Son.

Please review some of the names of Jesus:

- He is the King of Kings and Lord of Lords.
- Jesus is the first and the last; Alpha and Omega. He is the beginning and the end.
- Jesus is the King eternal, immortal, invisible.
- He is Captain of the Lord's Host.
- He is the King of glory.
- Jesus is the Lord strong and mighty; the Lord mighty in battle.
- He is the Lord which is, and which was, and which is to come.
- He is the Creator of the heavens and the earth.
- He is the Creator of all flesh.

This is the God we serve. Jesus Christ, our Lord and risen King. Jesus said, "I am He who lives, and was dead, and behold, I am alive forevermore. Amen. And I have the keys of Hades and of death."

Jesus promised His disciples that He would not leave them comfortless, but would send His Holy Spirit to lead and guide them (and us) into all truth. Below are some of the names of the Holy Spirit:

- Holy Spirit
- Spirit of Truth
- Spirit of Fire
- Spirit of Grace
- Spirit of Wisdom
- Spirit of Understanding

- Spirit of Counsel
- Spirit of Power
- Spirit of Power
- Spirit of Knowledge
- Spirit of the Fear of the Lord

Now that we know who we are and who Jesus is, we are equipped and ready to engage in this great spiritual warfare.

CHAPTER 8
BATTLE STRATEGIES

Soldiers do not engage in without a battle plan; neither should we. Throughout biblical history, God provided strategic battle plans for His people to gain victory over the enemy. God is doing the same thing today. For every circumstance that we face in life, He has a plan of victory. Jesus will never send us into a battle that we cannot win! Below, are a few examples of battle stratagems:

Stand still and see the salvation of the Lord. The Lord does not want us to worry about anything. He just wants us to stand still in our minds and see or behold God's salvation. Envision your victory. See your deliverance. Think on things that are lovely and true. Don't focus on the winds and forces of life. Rest in the Lord and wait patiently for Him. Don't allow your heart to be agitated or filled with fear.

Another strategy used to defeat the enemy is praise, worship, and obedience. This strategy literally tears down the strongholds of the enemy. Jericho is a good example of how praise, worship, and obedience effectively tore down strong holds. Jericho was a walled city, and an impenetrable fortress, but it could not withstand the praise, worship, and obedience to a living God. When God commanded the army of Israel to give a great shout on the seventh day of circling the city, the walls fell flat! Honor God through your praise, worship, and obedience and watch the walls of hurt, fear, and oppression come tumbling down.

The Bible says, "We are overcome by the blood of the Lamb and the words of our testimony." Because of the blood of the Lamb, Christ, we have access to come boldly before the throne of God and petition heaven for our needs (Ephesians 2:13). Because of the shed blood of Christ, our sins are forgiven (Matthew 26:28). The blood of Christ affords us to overcome Satan, the accuser of saints everywhere. The blood of Christ is our protection against the devourer. The word says, when I see the blood, I will not suffer the destroyer to enter into your homes (Exodus 12:13). In addition to applying the blood of Christ to all areas of our lives, we must testify what the word says about our situations.

An illustration of this strategy was used when David killed Goliath. Before David ever drew one rock against Goliath, he testified to the giant and told him, "You come against me with sword and spear and javelin, but I come against you in the name of the LORD Almighty, the God of the armies of Israel, whom you have defied. This day the LORD will deliver you into my hands, and I'll strike you down and cut off your head. This very day I will give the carcasses of the Philistine army to the birds and the wild animals, and the whole world will know that there is a God in Israel. All those gathered here will know that it is not by sword or spear that the LORD saves; for the battle is the LORD's, and he will give all of you into our hands" (1 Samuel 17:45-47). David testified not only of the giant's defeat, but the defeat of the entire Philistine army. What about us? Let us speak the word of the Lord against every giant, strongman, and demonic spirit that comes against us. We need to decree and declare to the enemy that he is a defeated foe, and that no weapon formed against us shall prosper.

Fasting and praying is another mighty strategy that produces great victories. When the disciples of Jesus could not cast out the demon-possessed child, Jesus told them this kind comes out only by fasting and praying. When someone has been under the influence of the devil for a long time, he does not want to be cast out. But out he must go at the name of Jesus! Fasting and praying stopped Esther's enemy, Haman, from destroying an entire race of people! God is the same yesterday, today, and forever. He is still giving His people the victory over the enemy.

CHAPTER 9
ANATOMY OF PRAYER

Before exercising any prayers or decrees, acknowledge who God is; always give Him His props. He is worthy of all praise. Confess your sins, repent of both known and unknown sins, and ask the Lord to forgive you and cleanse you from all filthiness of the flesh and spirit. Make sure that you forgive those who have sinned against you or hurt you. Now you are ready to come boldly before the throne of grace to obtain mercy and grace to help in time of need. Make your request made known unto God, and pray His word back to Him. Agree with His word, trust and believe that you already have the desired petitions. End the prayer with thanksgiving for God hearing and answering your prayers.

CHAPTER 10
PRAYERS FOR VARIOUS SITUATIONS

Warfare Prayer

Heavenly Father, You alone are God of all the kingdoms of the earth; You have made heaven and earth. I acknowledge and confess that Jesus is my Lord and Savior. I serve and honor the only true and living God. Thank You, Father for the blessings of life and peace bestowed upon me daily. Thank You for Your love and kindness. I repent of all sin, both known and unknown. Please forgive me, Lord. Wash me and cleanse me from all filthiness of the flesh and spirit. Create in me a clean heart, and renew a right spirit within me. Lord, Your word says, that if I confess my sins, You are faithful and just to forgive me and cleanse me from all unrighteousness. I also forgive those who have transgressed against me or hurt me. I bless them now in the name of Jesus and release them. Jesus, You said, "Whatsoever I bind on earth shall be bound in heaven, and whatsoever I loose on earth shall be loosed in heaven. Lord, You know all about this situation I am going through. Holy Spirit, please give me wisdom and revelation to pray effective, bulls-eye prayers that will turn this situation in my favor. In the name of Jesus, I bind Satan and any principalities, powers, rulers of darkness of this world, and spiritual wickedness in high places that come against me. In the name of Jesus, I bind the strongman of _____ along with any roots, fruits, tentacles, and weapons from operating in my life. In the name of Jesus, I command you and any cohorts to take up your weapons and leave my home, children, and _____ right now and do not come back. In the name of Jesus, I bind you from sending any replacements. In the name of Jesus, I bind every negative word ever spoken over my life. In the name of Jesus, I render those words powerless, void, untrue, and of no effect in my life. In the name of Jesus, I decree, declare, and testify by the blood of the Lamb that I am loosed now and forever from Satan and any principalities, powers, rulers of darkness of this world, and spiritual wickedness in high places that come against me. In the name of Jesus, I am loosed from the strongman of _____ and any of his roots, fruit, tentacles, and weapons. He whom the Son has made free is free indeed. No weapon formed against me shall prosper. Jesus, Your word says, "And they overcame Satan by the blood of the Lamb and the word of their testimony." In the name of Jesus, by the blood of the Lamb, I testify that I have been made forever free by Jesus Christ of _____, _____, etc.

Scriptures

Psalm 47:7
1 John 1:9
Psalm 51:10
Matthew 18:18-20
Isaiah 54:17
John 8:36
Revelation 12:11

Prayer Against Loneliness and Fear

Father, I feel so alone and afraid. There is not a single person in my life that I can comfortably share my situation with. I am trying so hard to be strong. I wear a mask of bravado, but inside I'm weak, broken, and desperate. Please heal the wounds of my soul. I will lift up my eyes to You because You are my help. You are my refuge and strength. Shine Your light in the dark places of my soul. Let Your salvation deliver me. I refuse to fear because You are with me. You will never leave me nor forsake me. Father, in the name of Jesus, banish every spirit of loneliness and fear. Grace me with Your presence and let Your joyous, perfect love flood my heart.

Scriptures:

> Psalm 46:1
> Psalm 27:1
> Psalm 23
> Hebrews 13:5
> John 4:18

Prayer for Overcoming the Past

Father, in the name of Jesus, please heal my broken heart and bind up my wounds Please help me to see beyond the pain I am feeling. Help me to see beyond my present circumstances. Throughout the day, my mind is revisiting the past. I'm often reminded of how someone hurt or betrayed me. Help me to stop buying tickets to vacation in my past. Every time I revisit my past, it costs me my peace, my joy, and my hope. Release me from past hurts, injustices, betrayals, and afflictions. Everything I see is colored through lenses of pain and regret. Heal my eyes that I may behold wonderful things out of Your law. Open my ears that I might hear and heed Your voice. Heal my entire being from venomous words spoken over my life. Deliver me from wounds of unforgiveness, roots of bitterness, and a false self-image. Close and seal every door of darkness and affliction in my life. Please forgive me and cleanse my whole body, soul, and spirit from all unrighteousness, sin, sickness, and disease. Bring me health and cure, and cure me; reveal to me the abundance of peace and truth. Help me to realize that I am a new creature in Christ Jesus. Help me to remember that old things are passed away, and all things become new. Father, in the name of Jesus, please grant me these petitions, supplications, and prayers according to Your word. Amen.

Scriptures:

Psalm 147:3
Jeremiah 33:6
Psalm 119:18
John 10:27
1 John 1:9
2 Corinthians 5:17

Breaking Free from Post-Traumatic Stress Disorder
Dear Father, I've experienced some traumatizing things in my past. No matter how hard I try to break free from reliving the terrible images in my mind, the fear, anxiety, dread, and infirmity seems hard-wired in my thoughts, feelings, and behavior. Your word says that You are the same yesterday, today, and forever. Please remove recurring, negative images in my mind that depict me as weak, vulnerable prey to my past. Take away the overwhelming feelings of panic, despair, and hopelessness. You created times and seasons. You are God over my yesterdays, my today, and my future. You are God over all my times and seasons. Father, in the name of Jesus, please visit my yesterdays and address the root of my fear, anxiety, dread, and infirmities. Please visit those times and seasons of my yesterdays that left me wounded and crippled in my spirit. Visit

those evil spirits that have oppressed me for so long. Destroy them with double destruction. Cause them to die and live no more. Bless me to forget my misery as waters that pass away. Isaiah 26:14 says, "They are dead, they shall not live; they are deceased, they shall not rise: therefore, hast thou visited and destroyed them, and made all their memory to perish." Cause the memory of the provoking trauma to cease. In the name of Jesus, I command every strongman of fear, anxiety, dread, evil foreboding, and infirmity to get out of my life. Jesus, in Your name, please shut and seal every demonic doorway that is used as an inroad into my life. In the name of Jesus, I apply the blood of the Lamb to the doorposts of my heart. In the name of Jesus, I curse every demonic tree in my life from the root and command it to die and bring forth no more fruit. In the name of Jesus, I break every ungodly soul tie. I have been delivered from the kingdom of darkness and have been translated into the kingdom of Jesus. I seal this prayer by the blood of the Lamb in the matchless name of Jesus.

Scriptures:

Jeremiah 17:18
Isaiah 26:14
Job 11:16
Revelation 12:11
Mark 11:20-24
Colossians 1:13

Unexpected Storms

Father, I don't understand why I am going through this storm, but somehow, it is working for my good. Through this furnace of affliction, You have prospered me to grow stronger. As I journey through this process, I refuse to fret or become anxious. I choose to rest patiently in You and wait upon Your deliverance. You are my provider and Your ears are open unto the voice of my cry. You have surrounded me with songs of deliverance, and my meditation of You is sweet. Give me wisdom, revelation, and direction in how You want me to proceed. I know that You are with me and will never leave me nor forsake me. Speak to the waves and winds of this storm and cause there to be a great calm in Jesus' name. Amen.

Scriptures:

Romans 8:28
Psalm 37:1
Philippians 4:19
Psalm 34:15
Psalm 104:34

Prayer for God's Vengeance and Vindication

Heavenly Father, the earth is Yours and the fullness thereof and everything that dwells therein. You are the Creator of all flesh. Your eyes are in every place beholding the good and the evil. You see the injustice and the plots of the enemy. Please avenge me of mine adversary. Let Your kingdom come into this situation; let Your will be done on earth as it is in heaven. I have no power of my own to fight against this great company of enemies. You told me that vengeance is Yours and You will repay. You said in Psalm 146:7-9 that You execute justice for the oppressed. Oh Father, execute judgment against satanic principalities, powers, rulers of darkness of this world, and spiritual wickedness in high places that have come against me and/or my family. Avenge me speedily. Let the angel of the Lord chase them, and let their way be slippery. Father, in the name of Jesus, let a consuming whirlwind of the Lord go forth with fury and bring pain and destruction upon the head of my enemy. In the name of Jesus, I speak death to ungodly soul ties in my life, my husband's life, my children's, and grandchildren's lives. I speak death to demons of oppression, sickness, sin, and disease and rid them out of my land now in Jesus' name. In the name of Jesus, I command every generational curse to be broken now! Jesus, in Your name, rain down Your snares, fire and brimstone, and bring a horrible tempest upon the head of my spiritual enemies. Execute double destruction upon the enemy who oppresses me. Arise oh Lord, disappoint him, cast him down: deliver my soul from the wicked. Deliver me from wicked men and women. Stop the floods of injustice carried out by ungodly men and women against me. Lift up a standard against the enemy. Fight against those who fight against me. Break the teeth in their mouths, and break out the fangs of the young lions. Break their arms of power, and remove them from their high places. Take up shield and buckler and deliver me. Do not let me be put to shame, but let my enemies cover themselves with shame. Do not let them perform their wicked devices. Restore unto me the years that the worms have eaten. Open up the windows of heaven and pour me out a blessing that I won't even have room enough to receive. Prepare a table before me in the presence of my enemies. Bless me to dwell securely in the land.

Scriptures:

Psalm 24:1
Psalm 21:11
Luke 18:7
Joel 2:25

Anxiety

Father, in the name of Jesus, I have been so worried about my situation, and I don't know how to stop worrying. My strength feels as though it is ebbing away. Please renew my spirit. Cause me to soar on eagle's wings, and let victory meet me at every step. Fill me with Your consistent, unshakeable peace in my body, soul, and spirit.

Let Your peace and strength flood my body, soul, and spirit like a torrential force of rain driving out all worry and fear in Jesus' name I pray, Amen.

Scriptures:

Isaiah 40:31
Isaiah 41:2
2 Thessalonians 3:16
Psalm 46:1
Philippians 4:6

Friendly Fire (Wounded by Loved Ones)
Dear Jesus, I can deal with my enemies hating me without a cause, but the things that hurt me most are the sharp arrows hurled at me by the people in my own house. Lord, I forgive them. Please heal the wounds hidden within the deepest corridors of my heart. Let Your blood cleanse me of poisonous words, bitterness, unforgiveness, and revenge. Fill me with Your love, and help me to love and forgive them. In Jesus' name, Amen.

Scriptures:

Psalm 41:9
Psalm 55:12-13
Matthew 5:44

Now, we are fully equipped with the whole armor of God to fight the good fight of faith. We are armed with the word of God, covered by the blood of Jesus, and His presence is with us. Begin to possess your Promised Land by framing your world with the word of God.

64486139R00033

Made in the USA
Middletown, DE
13 February 2018